True Romance

Thank you for destroying my Life

Vera Mygdala

ffmovement.org

The texts I share are always based in my own experience and observations. By no means I am claiming this to be the ultimate truth. I encourage everyone to find their own truth and to be open to it changing as new information integrates. As this is universal wisdom of us ALL, I do not claim any copyright. Feel free to utilize and share, as long as you keep the text complete as it is so it keeps its energetic signature. Thanks Vera

This book is dedicated to YOU. Yes YOU!
The brave lover and explorer, moving forward into the
depth of your own being, exploring your inner world in this
adventure called life, to find the key to TRUE ROMANCE.

"Love is the one thing we are capable of perceiving that transcends dimensions of time and space. Maybe we should trust that, even if we cannot yet understand it."
Interstellar

CONTENTS

PREFACE

This book is written for the brave ones. The real heroes that are not afraid to look into the mirror. The ones who are ready to surrender, to return to their innocence, and embrace vulnerability as a true strength.
For those that thought they had found true love, just to be ripped apart and having the floor pulled away under their feet. For those that no longer try to find answers outside, no longer are paying a lot of money for coaches, tarot readers, or any other self-proclaimed love experts to tell them what they want to hear, but facing the brutiful truth: You are the answer and you are the only one who can get yourself out of this crazy ride.

True Romance is not for the faint of heart. A true romance destroys your life and with it all beliefs you ever thought to be true. It rudely awakens you from a dream you thought was real. It deconstructs the fairytales you took for granted, about a prince and a princess that live happily ever after. It teaches you that the life you have been living until now was not the life you came here to live.

True Romance gives you a lot of tough love and causes a lot of pain. It leaves you speechless many times and twists your mind into such a confusion, that you don't know anymore what is right or wrong. Although this feels like the biggest punishment in that moment, it is actually a door-opener into a different reality. It strips you naked, it leaves you empty - so you can make space for

a whole new life to live.
A life in true freedom and empowerment, filled with joy shared with others, who have broken free from the chains of conditional love and life as well.

This book is not a self-help book. It is not trying to sell you a truth, it is simply a transformational device that supports you in relating your experience and discovering your blind-spots. It gives you the sign posts to come to a more holistic view on your encounter. In simple terms - it is a tool to shift your perspective and shift your experience.

You don't need to read this book in a linear way. It is not a check-list of exercises to do or knowledge to achieve. It is not designed for the linear mind. It is written from my heart to yours.
You might find things that upset you first, things that trigger your current belief system. You might even dislike me for that. You might even burn it. That is perfect!

Go with your intuition. Throw it in a corner if you feel like it. Put it under your pillow.
Put it away, pick it back up. Hold on to it and let it go.
It contains a lot of information and many layers of understanding will reveal themselves to you, each time you read it. There is no time pressure in reading the whole thing at once. You might come back to it after a while and re-reading will take you to a whole new level you were not able to see before.

Why have I written this book? Because I want to support you in moving forward and not get caught up in old patterns and loops. I am interested in your empowerment, because you are important and you are making a difference in this world.
Yes, you!

I have written this book, because I know exactly how you feel. I have been there. After the most amazing, best, and most fulfilling week in my whole life, filled with love, happiness and peace, it was taken away from me. And it was ugly. I have never felt such an intense pain in my life before. I have never cried so much without any relief. I could not understand why on earth I was punished so much after having found the love of my life and the solution and answer to what was missing in my life.

I have been through all this suffering, ailing and the intense pain myself, had a lot of false hopes and dead end streets to experience, where I had to turn around and pick myself up again. I learned a lot in a very short time. And this is what I want to share with you - to show you that it does not have to take years to find happiness and inner peace. It depends greatly on you and your willingness to move forward. All you need is to understand a few basic dynamics and change your perspective on this connection. Your ego will give you a very hard time in the beginning accepting those "universal laws". But once you have managed to quiet down your little chatter box in your head, and you see through the mind fog right onto the heart & soul level - everything becomes easier with each and every day.

One intention of this book is to give you context from the metaphysical/energetic point of view. It supports in giving you some peace of mind, and to know that you are not crazy and not alone. Another intention is to give you the bigger picture of the purpose of your experience. In between you will find useful tips to navigate with more ease.

Enjoy, explore, and discover a world beyond anything you could imagine!

MEETING THE ONE

You meet this person, look him or her into the eyes and are sucked in like by a tractor beam. The magnetic feeling is so intense – nothing you have ever experienced before. You know this is special. And you think: This is what I have been searching, what I have been waiting for my whole life. Now I am going to live happily ever after. I have found the person that makes me whole, the one that completes me. Right?

Nope! This magical encounter is not about romance in the first place, and we have to learn that the hard way. Especially in the beginning, when the just described bubble love phase ends abruptly. As magical as it feels, as devastating it becomes and in most cases is ending in a painful separation. As much as you would like to get over it, a challenging push and pull dynamic becomes the new normal. The harder you try to cut this person out of your thoughts, the more present s/he becomes. This person is in your thoughts and in your feelings 24/7, and there is nothing you can do to escape. It feels like going insane with all the fears and symptoms you are experiencing. You feel like you cannot survive without this other person. Your family and friends don't understand you and think you've gone completely bonkers. You are asking yourself more than once: "What is it that I have gotten into here, and why can I not let go of this?"

You start researching, because what is happening cannot be normal. Just to realize - that does not really help. There is so much information that circulates around. Soul Mates, Twin Flames, karmic partners, catalysts etc... and hundreds of offers and methods on how to get back together with the person you are so madly in love with. There you are - in the middle of this emotional chaos, feeling even smaller, shifting between despair and hope, asking yourself how you are supposed to survive even one more day with all this pain, these questions, these confusing feelings and in parallel - in an attempt to cope with it all - you try to find your way through the jungle of information on this topic, leaving you even more confused and helpless.

The mystical world of love has become an attractive market with some serious, but a lot more half-baked or even unserious offers and services, making money with the despair of people. And of course, it is beautiful, when those love experts tell you what you want to hear. That s/he is the ONE for you and you will end up being and sharing an amazing life together. You just gotta follow their program and advice you pay for, and you are on the right track. Until you reach a point where you realize: This is not the answer. I am in another loop.

Yes, it sucks. Big time. After the most amazing love explosion and so much joy and happiness, how can this be taken away from you? In such an ugly and painful way making you suffer so much and destroying the thing called life you used to have. Crying so many tears without relief and seeing no way out, not knowing how to function properly, despite all the promising words of the love experts. It feels like you must be doing something wrong because you are punished so much after having found the love of your life and the solution and answer to all of what was missing in your life before. That person that you could be completely honest and be yourself with, the person you just had to look into the eyes to see the pure eternal love and wisdom reflecting back to you, the person you could lean on and share silence with. The person that just got you by looking at you, the person with which time and space dissolved and all there was was this intense magnetic pull between the two of you, someone you would never want to let go of again. And as tough as it sounds - that exactly is what needs to be done: Letting go.

Before we get to that in more detail, let's dive a bit deeper into the characteristics of a True Romance connection.

CHARACTERISTICS OF A TRUE ROMANCE

Connections that are of True Romance enter your reality in different ways. They all have the same purpose: and waking you up to
empower you. They are cracking your program and belief of co-
dependent relationships and the idea of needing a partner to feel
complete.

They have nothing to do with a usual way of falling in love, of dat-
ing, of feeling butterflies, and building a relationship. Despite the
diverse ways they manifest in your life, they all share some common characteristics:

You Know It Instantly And It Goes Very Deep

When you meet, you immediately know this is very special and
is something you have never experienced before. Being with that
person feels like heaven on earth, and the feelings are so overwhelming and so intense that you forget everything else that
used to be important in life, including your own family! It just
seems you have known this person forever. You feel at home. You
are not playing games of showing your best version, dressing up,
trying to impress etc. No, it is a feeling of deep connection and
understanding, a love beyond anything you knew. You are open
and honest with each other, go into profound conversations,
and share your darkest secrets and feelings without any shame
although you hardly know each other. You feel completely ener-
gized, you hardly need any sleep or food and you feel a long lost
feeling of belonging and being home.

You Know Your Life Will Never Be The Same Again

After the encounter, you just know that your life will never be
the same again. For the first time in your life, you feel that you

are really alive and loving, not only existing and functioning. You feel seen, loved and appreciated for who you are, not for what you could be useful for.

You know that you cannot go back to "normal", living a lie and living up to others expectations. You feel free, independent and empowered with this person.

Until it happens, and the beauty of love turns around into what seems to be a nightmare. This connection destroys your old life and leaves you completely baffled not understanding how this all happened so quickly and you feel very alone, either because you ran for the hills - afraid of the intensity, or your partner left you unexpectedly and pushed you away.

You Are Pushed Into A Transformational Ride On Speed

This encounter triggered something deep within you. Something beyond all conditioning you grew up with and learned during your life. It is a glimpse of a remembrance, a feeling of something much bigger than what you thought life and your reality was. Your whole perception and experience of your surroundings shifts. You feel firey and uncomfortable energy rushes through your body and you become very sensitive to energy emitted from people and things in your surroundings. Being in public spaces becomes very uncomfortable, and you feel like hunkering down at home and you become very introverted. It can feel like listening to 20 songs at the same time when in a room full of people, and it can be very overwhelming. Like an infant catching all kinds of diseases, you don't have an active energetic immune system yet, meaning your (energetic) body has not learned yet to distinguish and has not developed any filters yet. You are experiencing deep dark depression, as all of your suppressed emotions surface and end up in lots of screaming and crying. Your cravings are changing, there is a longing to be in nature and quietness, your food intake is different, as you are all of a sudden very sensitive and allergic to many things you used to consume.

You See The Bigger Picture

After the big breakdown, when everything falls apart and you sit alone with the shards of your old live comes the breakthrough. You start seeing the bigger picture, and that this experience is much more than a romantic love story. The more you release old conditioning and belief systems, the more you make space for new information to be integrated. You start understanding the place of unity consciousness - that one mind that scientists and artists describe they connect to when they are getting their insights and inspirations. All of a sudden you know things that you have never read or learned anywhere before. You realize that this encounter was a catalyst, triggering an awakening and an expansion of your consciousness to remember who you truly are. Your authentic self, your essence, your value and your contribution. You realize that through this experience, you are connecting to others who share a similar story. More and more, you rediscover fun, playfulness, fellowship and connection. You become more and more self-sourcing in your energy, not needing others approval or attention to feel good. Step by step you understand that this was preparing you for what is to come. To inspire a shift in consciousness for other people, to remember their own essence and brilliance.

The Person Stays In Your Field No Matter What

Even after you have become completely self-sourcing in your energy, and you have found your inner equilibrium, your True Romance stays in your field. What was so painful before, this neverending, persisting presence in your thoughts and feelings, has shifted into pure, unconditional love, without any strings attached. What felt destructive before, is now fueling your being and feels good and motivating. The neediness has been replaced with unconditional sharing, there is no more need to be together or to be in touch. The love simply is.

DIFFERENT TYPES OF TRUE ROMANCE CONNECTIONS

These True Romances can happen in very different ways and can be categorized in a way that summarizes the many different stories of how they come into your reality. Each story is unique, but follows the same "software" or "energetic pattern", that creates the individual experience. This means they follow the same dynamics, yet can be of very different content and setup, depending on the individual energetic makeup / human design / gene keys. Each story has their specific timing and rhythm, so it is useless and counterproductive to compare with others. Here are the different main types of how the connections form.

No Separation Phase At All

This set up is the least common, as it is very draining and challenging for both partners involved. Despite the intense push and pull caused by the inner imbalance of masculine and feminine energies (we will get to that in more detail), the pair stays together, in most cases have children and work through the process together. Often, these pairs do not know for years or even decades what they are experiencing and why their relationship is so challenging and draining despite the huge love they feel for each other. All their energy and resources are spent on somehow maintaining the balance, as they do not understand that it is about finding balance within themselves first. They are so busy with each other, that they do not participate much in social activities. They are not aware of the bigger picture and are struggling through life and their relationship, trying to make it work based on an old template for relationships that does not match their energetic signature. Once they wake up to the bigger truth, they find their inner balance and are able to handle the connection in a different way.

They are shifting from fighting, judging and blaming each other, to appreciating and understanding each other and the dynamics at play. They start giving each other space, trusting each other and are not taking things personally anymore. They support each other into authenticity and freedom. They shift from co-dependency to interdependency. Step by step, they learn to surf the waves together instead of crashing individually and become inspiring and shining examples of an empowered and conscious couple.

Getting Back Together After A Short Separation Phase

There is quite a number of True Romance couples out there, many of which choose to be a coach and love expert on the topic. Although promising, because they already made it, daily life looks differently behind the scenes. Often enough, there is a large gap between the rose coloured world that is sold to their actual reality. Thankfully there are other couples who share openly about this very intense and challenging experience. Let's put it that way: Yes, they are living together, but that does not mean that they are two whole beings with an inner equilibrium unconditionally sharing a life with each other. No, they are still going through a lot of push and pulls and daily struggles, pushing each other's buttons. Usually there are major issues and challenges in other areas of their lives, be it health, money, purpose...

It is quite common that they mostly have troubles of being physically separate from each other and are experiencing great feelings of dependency and longing when the other one is gone. They usually don't have a social life outside of their bubble. That is why they also work together and have a business together.

These True Romance couples are important for the truth seekers out there. First, they represent the carrot of a possible reunion, and later the insight, that this is not it yet, either.

On And Off And On And Off

This setup is quite common. A lot of pairs are coming together and separating again, continuing to do so - going through cycles of drama and fear. They can neither be with nor without each other. The result is intense togetherness for a while, often including intense sexual experiences, just to fall apart again and going through longer and shorter periods of separation. They are doing the balancing on the go, getting together to trigger each other again into the next phase of separation and integration. Most of their energy goes into the balancing of the connection, especially in their time together, they seek the balance from outside through the partners. The separation phases serve to switch to finding their individual inner equilibrium and their essence. Some of them stay together as an empowered conscious couple, others continue their journey physically apart.

Permanent Separation

This type of connection seems to be the toughest one at first, but turns out to be the smoothest in the end. These pairs separate after the amazing bubble love phase, and are most often not even talking to each other anymore. If at all, they remain being casual friends and chat or meet from time to time. Just to get the next buttons pushed for the next level of releasing and growing. These True Romance connections usually serve as intense catalysts to catapult the individuals (or most of the time just one of them) into their rapid awakening and expansion of consciousness. While the metaphysically more feminine part (which is not gender related - we will go into detail on this later on), often already sees very clearly what this connection truly is about, the metaphysically more masculine part remains "asleep" and continues living his/her life as before. The intense connection is mostly remembered as an intense sexual attraction that has just faded away. Once they are back in touch again after a long first period of silence, the masculine usually defines this connection as "friendship only". S/he just cannot feel the connection in the same way, as they are not tuned into the same energetic frequency and are not able to hold that frequency for long. In these True Romance connections, bi-polarity is cooking high, and the feminine feels as if s/he is dealing with two different persons that are not even aware of each other. In earlier phases that leaves them completely confused, as words and actions differ so much. Although it seems very hurtful from the human perspective to be in separation, and getting a friendship talk, from an energetic perspective, it is the quickest way to move forward and finding inner balance and wholeness, simply because there are no distractions through the partner.

Metaphysical Connection First

This type of connection is the most challenging and uncanny one to the human mind, as it is something that seems impossible. The human mind believes in and is conditioned with the idea of separation, that we are individual humans with our own thoughts and body. The moment this form of True Romance happens, your mind and the mind of people around you go into complete denial mode. "This cannot be! You are crazy! It is impossible!" Nevertheless, you feel like you have fallen deeply, madly in love with a person you have never met and you are mostly looked at with pity, as someone being hopelessly infatuated with a celebrity that is completely out of reach for you. The connection is happening on the metaphysical/energetic level. The level of the one mind/ unity consciousness, where everyone is connected to everything.

Physicists call it the Quantum Field, the spiritual world would talk about the ether.
In this type of connection, the energetic experience is a lot more intense than for pairs that have met in the physical.

Looking at all types of connections, it is obvious that the dynamics are always the same. All of them are challenging, exhausting and draining first, dealing with the inner imbalance of the individuals, until the individual decides to move on from the loops of this tiring push and pull dynamic, focus on themselves and getting their own "house in order". A healthy interdependent, unconditional, loving connection only becomes possible when the individuals have worked their way out of co-dependency patterns, expectations and attachments, and have transformed into self-loving, empowered, independent individuals. No matter if they are in touch with their partners, even living with them or are not communicating at all, the key is the same: You are completely happy and fulfilled alone, and you don't miss or need to be with your partner anymore. You can even be with another person, living and loving unconditionally.

THE RUNNING AND CHASING GAME

A dynamic that usually plays out in a True Romance connection is that of running and chasing. One of the two runs for the hills, while the other chases after him/her. It seems so frustrating that something that felt so good ends up in such a weird dynamic. Everything we had learned about relationships and how you treat each other simply seems to not apply in these connections. Why is this the case?

In order to understand this on a deeper level, we need to go beyond the stories. We are going to have to look into the process of creation and how the laws of physics / the laws of the universe are always working.

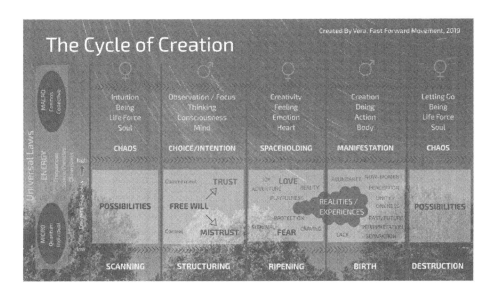

In the beginning is chaos. The metaphysical sea of possibilities we swim in is of feminine nature/energy. She (not gender based) - our intuition - does nothing but float in this sea and is scanning all possibilities, while being open to all options. She feels intuitively what resonates and what feels good. When we look into the string theory, this is when photons are still wave patterns. This is the moment when synchronicities take place. When alike wave patterns align with alike wave patterns. Yet - nothing happens as long as she just floats. Until the metaphysical masculine joins in and starts observing and focusing on a possibility. The photon becomes a particle. It takes a (thought) form. He starts structuring the chaos, to then make a choice, setting an intention. Instead of spraying the energy everywhere, the metaphysical masculine bundles the energy and co-creates powerful momentum with the metaphysical feminine.

This choice can be made based on love or on fear, trust or mistrust. The difference: commitment (detached from a certain outcome) or control (an expectation). This choice impacts the whole manifestation of the individual reality/experience in the physical world.

This is the whole difference between the third and the fifth dimension. It is nothing but a difference in our own energetic frequency/vibration. Our own vibration defines what we align with. The experience of a true romance challenges us in a way to break down old frequency patterns of fear and shift into the frequency of unconditional love and ultimate trust.

Our own vibration defines what we experience in our outer reality: abundance, unity and ease, or lack, separation and effort. We enter the embodiment process as the spiritual masculine's intention kicks off the earthly embodied flow in form of an emotion to truly feel the creation ripening. This is the earthly feminine taking over. The moment an emotion is felt, we are truly dedicated to the experience we chose. That can be based on trust, or on mistrust!

Creativity is initiated. We are pregnant with an idea or project. The evolved earthly feminine is patient and fully trusts that everything comes together in perfect timing. Once the idea or project is ripe and ready to be born, the earthly masculine takes over again. Now it is time for action, for physical manifestation.

Looking at this, it becomes obvious that we all need to find this inner flow, trust and balance first to become powerful creators and manifestors. We all have our deficiencies and energetic imbalances that we are learning to shift in the course of this process to return to an inner equilibrium. When we shift from co-dependency (needing the energy of someone else to create) to independence (inner union and being fully re-connected to Source/ the ALL encompassing intelligence we are all an aspect of), we are preparing for interdependence - empowered individual self-sourcing aspects of the ONE organism, sharing unconditionally, and amplifying each other.

Here you see that the old ways of partnerships are always ending up in fear cycles. True Romance is an experience that is designed for you to become a powerful, self-sourcing aspect that is then reuniting in a healthy interdependence with a partner and more people, to co-create in completely new, unknown ways.

When looking at this process, you can also see that the spiritual feminine (again, it is not gender related, but energetically speaking) goes through that process first. Simply because it is the nature of this Universe. A strong intuition is the basis for everything else to come. Only those that are able to see and feel all possibilities can initiate the necessary shifts to create a new reference point for others to follow.

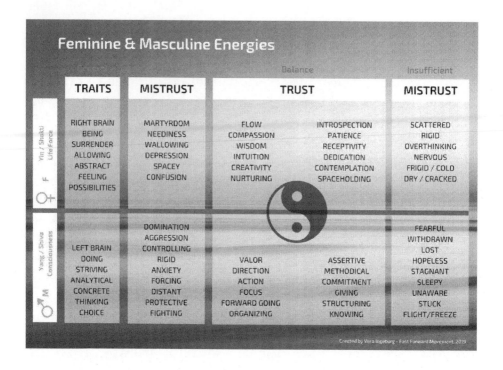

Now having learned this, how does this apply to your True Romance? You share one energetic field with your partner, but you have decided for an overproportional unequal share of energies before incarnating. This way, you made sure, you would gravitate towards each other to find each other again to initiate the earthly human process of ascension / embodiment of Oneness.

You made sure to feel such an intense pull towards each other to stay motivated to go through this process individually. As beautiful as it feels in the beginning, it becomes overly challenging. Your energetic and physical bodies are not able yet to channel this huge amount of energy, and with the old set-up for duality, you automatically suck/pull energy from each other. There is nothing wrong with that - everyone in duality (the third dimension) operates that way. That dimension was set up to steal energy from each other. We all do it in that realm. Until we shift out of it, and our bodies transform.

So here we are, pulling energy from each other in our true

romance, where we each have our deficit. Intense longing and missing on the one end, intense need for protection and shutting down on the other. Both trying to apply their inner child strategies to get love and prevent pain.

The more feminine tries everything to get the energy to satisfy the longing and missing, while the masculine goes into a more passive sucking mode. By shutting down his/her heart, s/he remains in the old reality and does not remember the incredible heart to heart connection. Most often, they confuse the memory with an intense sexual connection/attraction that has died down as this is the closest reference point they have from their old experience. They have to shut down completely - as it is the only way for the more feminine to let go of trying to get the energy from their partner, and instead starting to shift into empowerment and self-sourcing through intense emotional releases and many painful breakdowns (of old beliefs, stories and conditioning) and breakthroughs.

Feminine & Masculine Energies - Details

	General Traits	Excess	Balance	Insufficient
SPIRITUAL FEMININE	• Translated through the heart • Flow • Love • Chaos • Possibility • Scanning • Abstract • Feeling	• Martyrdom • Neediness • Spacey	• Intuition • Compassion • Contemplating • Introspection	• Overthinking • Nervous • Scattered
SPIRITUAL MASCULINE	• Translated through the crown • Conscisouness • Light • Concrete • Focus • Structuring • Analytical • Choice	• Controlling • Distant • Anxiety • Forcing	• Focus • Commitment • Methodical • Direction	• Fearful • Withdrawn • Unaware • Lost
EARTHLY FEMININE	• Embodied through right brain • Being • Allowing • Dedication • Surrender • Creativity	• Confusion • Depression • Fleeing • Freezing	• Patience • Receptivity • Nurturing	• Rigid • Cold • Dry
EARTHLY MASCULINE	• Embodied through left brain • Doing • Striving • Creation • Action • Manifestation	• Rigid Ideas • Protective • Fighting • Aggression	• Forward Going • Organizing • Assertive • Giving • Valor	• Hopeless • Sleepy • Stagnant • Stuck

Created by Vera Ingeborg - Fast Forward Movement, 2019

On a sidenote, the individual energetic mix is different for each couple. The most extreme ones would be what humans would label as a psychopath on the one end (95% spiritual and earthly masculine, extremely conscious and a real doer, but not able to feel emotions or having any patience), and the cardio-empath on the other extreme (95% spiritual and earthly feminine, extremely intuitive, sensitive and creative, but not able at all to focus, to take decisions or get things done).

In between there are many different options and set ups in terms of distribution of energies and combinations of energetic set ups. There are couples that connect more earthly / sexually / physically first and discover a connection and flow there as never before, but they truly struggle with communicating with each other. That shows that they decided for a strong sexual polarity first, but not having established a mental connection yet. And there are couples that have an amazing mental clock, being able to share and talk for hours, yet having sex with each other is downright impossible. The only thing all pairs share is the heart to heart connection.

This should make it clear why the individual experience of a true romance differs and varies widely and is not the same for everyone.

Let's go back to the running and the chasing phenomenon.

In many cases, the more spiritual feminine is more earthly masculine, and the more spiritual masculine is more earthly feminine. While the spiritual feminine aches to be with the partner, her strong immature earthly masculine desperately wants to make it happen and fights for it (chasing).

He/she is not (yet) able to stay focused on her own process (deficit of spiritual masculine) and has no patience to let things unfold naturally (deficit of earthly feminine energy).

The running on the other hand is a very feminine fear reaction of the immature earthly feminine (flight, freeze), getting into a place of not having to take action, but rather distract oneself by focusing on other projects (spiritual masculine), to not have to deal with all the possibilities with regards to the connection.

Only when we have all these parts back in a healthy equilibrium within, and the individuals are able to navigate the process of creation from a place of love independently, they are ready to enter a new phase of co-creation, based on interdependency. Then, it becomes a sharing and amplification of powerful, individual energies, instead of draining each other energetically.

The moment the spiritual feminine has found the inner balance, and has stopped pulling energy and providing energy, the process for the spiritual masculine can begin as s/he will start feeling the void, his/her world will fall apart, s/he will feel exhausted, incomplete and empty. It will become so uncomfortable at some point, that s/he will start finding ways into inner equilibrium as well.

FROM PROJECTIONS TO COMPASSION

What we learn in this whole process is to look into the energetic mirror. When we start out on this journey of a true romance, our mind tries to reference it to an experience it remembers. And it just cannot fit it into a box. It goes back to what it knows: Projecting. We are making the counterpart responsible for our pain, for our suffering. Our mind only knows judgment and blame. It cannot understand that the partner actually serves us as a mirror to see our own imbalance and shadows. That s/he acts with the intention (from a soul perspective) to set you free.

It takes guts to accept that all of this is happening for you, not to you, and that this is actually a fast-paced process for our individual liberation of our mind-prison.

How many times do you fall onto your knees, sobbing and screaming: "What's the fucking point!". You think you cannot live without the other, and they just don't seem to behave the way people should behave according to your value system and learned moral. No matter how hard you try, they just cannot be controlled or manipulated into a different behaviour.

You fall into darkness. One dark night of the soul follows the other, so much emotional stuff is coming up, and you just feel completely lost. You just want to die because life becomes meaningless and too painful to cope with. Why are you still here?
You are pushed over the edge of what you knew to be true, until you surrender. And you start to listen to a new voice that comes in. The whisper of your intuitive heart. With every cognitive dissonance and breakdown, comes a bit more wisdom and trust.

Step by step by step, your energetic frequency shifts, with every tear cried that you own as your own feeling and pattern, you transform. You learn a completely new way of looking at things. Through a higher lens of unconditional love that has nothing to do with what you had thought was love. You realize that conditional love was actually fear and attachment disguised as love.

Again and again, you learn to let go and let things be. You start to see the beauty and perfection in this pain. You see that True Romance is taking you back to the origins, to where you had created the fear patterns and belief systems in the first place. You learn to shift judgment into compassion, and blame into gratitude. You get more and more glimpses of unconditional love. Loving what is - in every moment - and seeing the perfection in it all!

You realize that there is a much bigger perspective and purpose from what you could see before.

As mentioned at the beginning, letting go is key to the inner process of shifting your frequency into unconditional love and universal trust.

But what does it really mean?

Well, first of all, as this is the shorter answer: What does it not mean?

It certainly does not mean to let go of your partner, as it is simply not possible. The energetic connection you share is eternal, and you cannot break it or cut it off. You cannot protect yourself from it, unless you want to continue to hurt yourself. The more you try to severe it for good, the more painful it gets. You will need to find a way, how to accept this connection, how to handle it and how to use the energy you share with each other in a productive way.

Here are some keys to letting go:

Let Go Of Your 3D Behavioural Patterns

Don't try to understand what is happening to you with your mind. It will only drive you crazy and create even more distance. Your ego-mind will try to understand and analyse this connection out of its third dimensional view (the dimension of separation and lack we have experienced as reality so far), and will continuously fail to do so. It will try to blame yourself, your partner and others, and will want to chase your partner because of the immense fear of loss and not being good enough it has. True romance is nothing to be understood, it is to be experienced. All of your suffering and pain comes from the ego and its conditioning, not from your soul. So don't get tired of putting your ego into the backseat. It is important though to not fight your ego but accept it. Unconditional love! It is only trying to do its job to protect you and it really does not know any better. Give your ego a name so you can talk to it and treat it like an ailing person, feeling compassion for it and at the same time being able to observe it. This way, you create a healthy distance as an observer, realizing this is not your true self being active. One day, you will realize that your ego surrendered and follows your heart/intuition. Your inner guidance is taking over. With every emotion you embrace, you allow to surface and express with unconditional love and compassion for yourself and your partner, instead of blame and judgement, your frequency shifts, and you feel lighter.

Let Go Of Attachments

In our life we are so unaware how many attachments we create out of a need for safety and value. Not only attachments to people, but also to things and contracts to somehow have a guarantee to be safe. Just start looking into your own set up of life - can you see those many attachments and co-dependencies you are carrying around?
Letting go of those can mean many things. Letting go of trying to please everyone. Of being afraid of consequences when we are really honest and express ourselves, letting go of all the stuff we hoard, letting go of a job that does not fulfill us, etc. True Romance strips you naked and takes away everything you thought was important. It turns your perspective upside down. Attachments are all those co-dependencies blocking us from unconditional love.

Let Go Of Any Need Of Control

It is important to understand that True Romances are not following the human idea of relationships. You are not in control. The universe is. In earthly terms we would say we go through an evolution. Your ego loves to control things, and to make things happen, to have an alleged secure environment. In trying to control this connection, all you do is wasting a lot of energy for nothing. This energy is much better redirected into other areas in your life, as for example your own health and transformation, and acts of kindness with people around you, learning unconditional sharing. All you can do is trust, relax and be patient and surrender to this process. Know that on a higher level your soul has prepared it exactly this way for you, so you can remember who you truly are. The only thing you can "control" are your own activities, emotions and attitudes. Focus on your own stuff and your own lessons. Don't resist or fight against anything that is happening "to" you. Accept it, look at it without judging it or identifying with it and let it pass through you. Tell yourself that these moments will pass and that this is your ego struggling. Become the observer, again and again. You will notice that these moments get less, and that you dissolve past patterns and behaviours, that you learn to love yourself, and that you start to feel more and more unconditional love for yourself and everything around you.

Let Go Of The Romantic Idea

A lot of stories about soul mates, twin flames and cosmic love out there romanticize the idea very much. That is far from the true experience. True Romance becomes possible once we have shed our old skin and patterns completely. The purpose of the connection is not a partnership as we know it, it is meant to liberate you and accelerate your awakening.

Accept and feel honoured to be an aspect of a much bigger picture you are starting to see and remember. This goes way beyond two people being madly in love. This is about catalyzing a shift for the whole planet. As much as your ego would like to hear it, there is no guarantee you will be together with your partner. It really depends on what serves best for the whole. You have to learn that you don't need your partner. Neediness is co-dependency, based on duality, the make up of the third dimension. Accepting this fact will help you immensely to move forward, and to develop and grow and open up for other possibilities that life might hold in future for you.

Of course, it does not mean to try to control and stop thinking about your partner either. Dream, recall memories, tap into that energy - it will motivate you to continue. At the same time - don't fall into victim mentality and dwell in self-pity.

Focus on your own growth, and expansion. Learn to enjoy the process. It is happening for you, not to you. Don't think about a goal of reunion, but celebrate the the little steps and achievements day by day of healing (remembering your wholeness), as well as the big and little lessons, glimpses, insights, epiphanies. This whole process is about your own empowerment and recognizing your vulnerability as your true strength.
Realize that you would not have developed and grown in such a short phase if your partner would have been there for you. And be proud of yourself!

Be grateful for this divine experience. A gratitude journal can support, writing down everything you are grateful for in this process. It takes a bit to change your perspective, but once you do, you will recognize that even the toughest moments are meant to serve and strengthen you and have their purpose.

Let Go Of Any Expectations

Our ego is trained to permanently expect something and create conditions. It cannot be unconditional, only our heart can.
Stop expecting anything in this connection, no matter if it is in terms of timing (as to whether and when they will get in touch) or reactions (whether they will feel bad or guilty about their behaviour) or their awakening process.
Your partner has his/her own process and needs to go through his/

her experience on his/her own in his/her own timing. There is nothing you can do or say directed towards them to speed up that process. Again - you cannot control it!

It is an internal process and it has its own speed. All you can do is working through your own things and hold space in your heart - feeling the unconditional love free from blame or regret. This will take pressure away from the connection and will help you to move on. Enjoy the fact that you are connected on the energetic level. Embrace this needy and control-freaky side of yourself without judgment or identifying with it. Give yourself some "rules", for example to check the phone only twice per day. Step by step attachments/expectations will dissolve until they are gone completely.

Let Go Of Your Victim Role

Understand that this is always about you. Don't blame your partner for the pain you are experiencing. He/she is just pushing the buttons needed to be pushed for your own evolution and growth. This connection bring up all past imprinted patterns, templates and fears that you are forced to take a look at. Your deepest shadows show up for transformation. You will learn what still wants to be seen. You will discover the potentials inside of you that want to be awakened. Facing and releasing your own fear and trauma is a big part of this connection. Deal with them, feel them and work on self-acceptance and self-love. Unconditionally embrace yourself! You cannot love anyone else unconditionally before you are able to love yourself in this way. Wholeness comes from within, no one else can do that for you. A relationship in the physical is an added benefit but nothing that will give you the feeling of being whole.

Write down how you see the situation out of your victim perspective and then again from the perspective (mind/ego) of the empowered version of you (soul/heart). Isn't the difference amazing?

Let Go Of Assumptions

Our mind loves to interpret the actions and behaviour of other people. Simply let go of it. It does not serve you at all, and just keeps you in looping fear patterns you are projecting onto your partner and the situation. You cannot know what is going on inside of your partner and why he/she is acting that way. Keep refocusing on what the behaviour triggers for you and process the emotion in a constructive way.

Let Go Of The Need To Know

One of the biggest 'lessons' True Romance brings us, is to be comfortable with what IS. Here and Now. Not wanting it different, wanting to escape it, wanting to distract from it, but truly learning to love what IS. That is unconditional love! It does not matter how much you read about your soul connection with the other person, how much oracle cards you read day by day, how many people/coaches you talk to. At some point you just need to accept that you cannot know. All you can do is to keep refocusing on what all of this brings for you, how much you are growing and evolving, how different you perspective on life becomes, how many new connections and friendships you make. Refocusing on loving what IS, instead of condemning the moment

Once you have accepted the higher purpose of this connection and you have decided to move on with life, you will most likely experience an awakening process "on speed". The metaphysical quantum world is starting to reveal itself to you. This is far from being comfortable. It can get very intense, dark and ugly as all of our inner demons show up for release. Be assured that this is perfectly normal and necessary. You will feel better eventually. You will go through periods of deep emotional cleansing. Your trauma, your survival strategies, your strategies to get attention, your stories you believed about yourself and the world.... They will all show up with full force so you can drop all that weight that keeps your frequency down and keeps you feeling small and unworthy. You will have extreme highs and lows and you will live your life on an emotional rollercoaster for a while. There will be times when you ask yourself how much longer you will be able to take this, and you will want all of this to just end.

True Romance triggers a shift in your energetic system, it blasts your heart and your channels wide open. You will probably experience all sorts of unfamiliar energy movements in your chakras that can feel very intense and even painful and very confusing. The so called Kundalini often gets activated and burns like fire through your system.
You will probably become very sensitive to other people's energies and emotions, especially those from your partner, and you will need time to develop energetic filters / a sort of energetic immune system, where your energetic bodies learn to discern what is relevant and what is not.
You might even be affected by EMF (electromagnetic fields), moon cycles or other natural events like earth quakes, extreme weathers, solar flares or human events such as mass panics.

When experiencing moments like this, it is very important to observe the energies closely to get more familiar with them. In order for our energetic system to evolve, we should not just close down and try to protect ourselves. We need to find our way to trigger our system without letting it get too much to handle.

There will probably be times of extreme fatigue when all you want to do is rest, and you will have all kinds of physical symptoms such as skin-breakouts, headaches, flu-like symptoms, joint-aches, nerves overfiring etc. Allow yourself to rest and be patient. It is nothing to be afraid of. Although it is happening in waves, and you might sometimes feel this is just a loop, you will feel better and better, as you raise your frequency step by step.

You will most likely notice that your body is changing, and you will have different cravings than you used to. Your body might reject anything you used to be attached to and you used to consume to compensate for pain. You will probably feel the need for a lot more alone and quiet time, and will want to be in nature for grounding.

Your whole body is upgrading for a new frequency!

With regards to your consciousness, you will most likely experience it expanding. You might even re-establish your connection into unity consciousness, your self-talk might increase, and you might all of a sudden know things out of thin air.

A whole new world and reality starts to open up, and it can feel scary and like you are losing it. It is completely normal to feel that way. You are basically waking up from the Matrix, a bad dream that was an illusion. Embrace what comes through, listen to it, it will make more and more sense over time. You are learning a new language: The one of energy and emotional intelligence, it is a language that you can only feel through your heart center.

On days you feel weak and down, take as much time for yourself as you can, be kind to yourself, sleep, relax, go outside for walks in nature, take a bath, write a journal, paint, listen to your favourite music - whatever feels calming and soothing for you in this moment.

It might help you to exchange with people who understand this connection. There are a lot of forums and groups on social media, who offer a safe space without selling anything. Family and friends, although they want to help you will not understand what you are going through and why you cannot detach from this connection, so their advice - although meant to make you feel better - has often the reverse effect and makes you rather sad or angry. It is just nothing you could explain to someone who has not experienced it.

You can practice to redirect energy into something creative, or into acts of unconditional kindness - even if it is just smiling at a stranger or complimenting a waiter in a cafe. This supports attuning to a higher frequency and triggering the release of the weight you no longer need to carry.

On days you feel great, celebrate it! Enjoy and be playful and use your energy to move forward with your life and purpose.
To summarize: Be patient with yourself and your partner when going through this awakening process. Hold a loving and compassionate space for them. They are just dealing with their trauma and pain, and are scared of losing control. Just as your ego is not surrendering over night, theirs is not either.

There is no guarantee for a reunion in this lifetime, but there is a guarantee that your life becomes lighter and more and more magical the more you focus on your own process.
Although your partner remains present in your energetic field, at some point it becomes normal, and is no longer upsetting or disturbing in any way. It just is, and you will notice that there is no need to do anything with that presence accompanying you. You can start interacting with it in a whole different, creative and constructive way.

"Bad" days will come and go and get less and less intense as you find back to your inner Source, self-love and the realization that you don't need your partner to complete you.

Don't forget: You are a human under construction, there will be ups and downs, because that is just the natural law of cycles. All you can do is working on keeping the cycles in a range that you can deal with and not trying to push things forward. We are learning to go with that flow. Once you realize that even the tough times are meant to serve and strengthen us, and as we learn to see the positive sides also in the perceived shitty moments, everything becomes easier.

When emotions come up: Observe, accept, don't judge or blame yourself or others and let it pass through you. Be kind to yourself even with anger. It is a powerful and fast energy that transforms a lot of energy in a short time when not directed towards anyone or anything, but just released.

Maybe it helps to see your life like watching your own Hollywood movie. You know thre will be a happy end, but you just don't know how it will all unfold. All you know that there will be bumps and plot turns along the storyline to keep it interesting. This way, your True Romance can even be fun!

THE METAPHYSICS

Moving beyond the human mind with its stories and drama, you can take a completely different perspective on our experience. It often helps to look into the energetic dynamics of it all. You are actually truly shifting dimensions! You are going from one perceived reality to another!

Especially in the beginning, we often mistake True Romance for a normal relationship and an intense romantic connection. It is nothing we have experienced before, yet our mind tries to relate it to something we know: Having fallen madly in love. That is not it.

True Romance has actually nothing to do with that and is the opposite of what we learned to be a good, beautiful and successful relationship. Everything, literally everything becomes a paradox!
Yes, there might be a reunion at some point, but the quicker we let go of the idea for now, the faster we move forward.

The often called "bubble love phase" in the beginning of the connection, when we get lost in space and time, when everything feels so perfect and beautiful becomes our personal bait, the carrot in front of our nose that keeps us going. It is the Universe giving you a glimpse of what True Romance feels like. A glimpse of heaven on earth. The fifth dimension and beyond. Before you get kicked back into your current reality (third dimension) to be confronted with and see and feel everything within you that is in the way of unconditional love.

It seems to be the cruellest thing to lose what you wanted and love most. You feel so left alone. Abandoned, unwanted and completely confused and devastated. You start chasing the other person or running away. You are searching for answers, stumble upon first articles on soul connections, twin flames etc. and are learning that this is different from what you have experienced before. You are kicked into a new world. Metaphysics, spirituality, more stories, more labels, more belief systems. It is too easy to get attached again - your ego just wants to find something to identify with. At least you are special now, because you are part of the 144.000, or on an important mission to save the planet!

All you want is this rollercoaster to end and be with that person! You would do anything. Put your hand on your heart for a moment. It is tough to accept that you fell for the next conditional trap.

Conditions are a product of our linear mind and human programming that if we do something there is a consequence - an outcome. "If this… then that." is a good way to detect when we are conditional. When we expect an outcome. In our case here: "I will be with that person if I do all the work, if I save the planet, if I blablabla."

Yes, it is tough to admit it. And even tougher to not judge ourselves for it! We are all learning to let go of all the conditional codependencies we have created. It is fine! Love yourself unconditionally. We all did not know any better or different until now. You are learning and evolving, nothing that happens over night!

Yes, you want to be with that person. You just don't know how, because your mind will try to go back to what it knows, and will try to find solutions for a problem that does not really exist! It cannot find the answer with anything it has learned and has been programmed with in the past, be it through societal conventions, education, school, church, the news, the governments, marketing etc. Any of it does simply not apply to this connection. True Romance is literally forcing you to drop all of it.

Your mind is trying its best, but it just cannot read and understand what is unconditional. It is beyond what it can perceive. The only place where you find your answers is in the heart. In the moment, here and now. That is the only place the mind cannot be at.

Every time you catch your mind going into past or future, bring yourself back to here and now. An easy way to do that is to focus on your senses. Focus on what you hear, sense, smell, taste and see right now. This automatically shuts down the mind and opens your heart. Connect with what is. The more you practice, the easier it becomes. Until it is your new normal and you don't really know anymore how to be not in the NOW.

THE PURPOSE OF TRUE ROMANCE

True Romance is a blessing in disguise. You become a radiant, shining lighthouse of unconditional love, and you inspire so much change in other people, just by being you, your true authentic self, sharing your essence, doing and sharing what you love with the world, and living your life differently to the current reality of most human beings. The freedom you become will draw people towards you that are in awe of your light and energy you emit. You are a natural leader, without having to lead anyone. It just happens.

Purpose 1: Your Empowerment

When you embark on the journey of True Romance, you are thrown into a process of true empowerment. Power has nothing to do with the old world view we have. It has nothing to do with control. In the mind-driven third dimension, we think we need to control and manipulate our outside world to survive and to be successful. That is the old power game. When you meet your True Romance, a process of remembering and deconditioning begins that takes you back to your origin. Your essence. Your Innocence. Before you learned fear and separation. Like an onion, you are unpeeling layers that are not you but masks you have worn to survive the old world.

True power comes from the inside out. In this process of empowerment you discover that your true power is your vulnerability. The more you shed stored emotion from your body, the more your emotional intelligence, your COMPASSion comes online. It is your full body intuition, that operates on trust and a deep inner knowing. The more you embody this power of love, the less fear can get a grip on you. You simply know that you are always right on track, and exactly where you are. By being this shining and radiant example of empowerment, other people will perceive you as courageous beyond measures. They will want to know your secrets, and are "energetically infected". You will start planting seeds everywhere so people can discover their own inner power. This way, you contribute to shifting humanity, just by being you.

Purpose 2: Connecting The Heart Grid

Nature and the Universe work always perfectly and accurately like a Swiss watch. Our mind does not want to believe that and thinks that we are separate from nature and its universal laws. The result is a humanity completely out of alignment with the cycles, following artificial linear structures and time. There is no way this could ever be in harmony and truly sustainable.

When you go on your search for answers, you connect with people who have similar experiences and understand what you are going through. You start connecting into the heart-grid (the grid of the fifth dimension) and you will meet people all around the planet. The heart grid is a completely alternative energetic connection beyond "the Matrix" (the mind grid). The heart grid unites people through their open hearts, while the matrix creates an illusion of separation. The matrix talks from mind program (belief) to mind program and creates more separation, opinions, disagreements, fights, wars etc. The heart grid communicates energetically, beyond any belief. People who start embodying unconditional love, life and sharing and living from the heart are amplifying the heart grid and inspire people who are still in the matrix to remember their essence and true self.

It is no coincidence that people with the experience of a True Romance are located strategically distributed all around the planet to weave and strengthen this web of love for a shift of humanity from mind (fear-based) to heart (love-based) living. That is how an organism in nature starts an evolutionary transformation. By cells being distributed in a way that it can shift in the most effortless and efficient way. Together, we are embodying Oneness and assist humanity in remembering that we are all aspects of the one organism, not only capable but actually designed for living and co-creating in harmony.

Purpose 3: Holding Space For Humanity

By being the embodiment of love, and living your life based on absolute trust, not compromising your essence, you automatically become a space holder for everyone who is going through intense disruption of their old life and transformation. You are being that beacon of light (people would interpret it as hope) that you bring in times of darkness. Together with all these other beautiful aspects around the world, you are holding that unconditional space of compassion without any judgment or blame. You see the innocent child in everyone that got wounded and just tried to survive and prevent pain. You can offer the feeling of truly being seen, loved and nurtured.
You bring calm and peace to someone who is going through the throws of their worst fears manifesting. You offer a safe container of love.

Purpose 4: Clearing The Whole Lineage

You are not only you and your trauma, you are carrying the trauma of your whole family lineage in your cellular memory. The more you have worked through your emotional memory of this lifetime, the more the cellular memory will come up for release. You will realize that you are releasing without any memory or story attached. It is just a feeling. This way, you are transforming your whole body into a new structure and design! You will be able to process a lot more high frequencies and expand your love around the whole planet!
Your body will literally look lighter and younger, it will be more agile and capable of living without food or water. It sounds im-

possible to the mind, but more and more people are experiencing this transformation. You are becoming a new human, witnessing evolution while you are alive!

Purpose 5: Introducing New Relationship And Family Templates

The more you anchor in unconditional love and True Romance, you will likely meet a partner (yes, it does not have to be the one you thought was the one...) that you will be with in a completely new way. Not co-dependent, but interdependent. Not needing each other, but wanting to share and co-create with each other.
Two whole beings amplifying each other instead of draining each other.
This way, you become a shining example for a completely new template for relating. The same happens for families. Everything changes when empowered beings are sharing their lives instead of making their happiness dependent on each other.
No contracts, no duties or obligations, no compromise on our individual essence. Instead, we value each other for who we are, not for what we could be useful for.
Children will grow up trauma free and are seen in their essence and appreciated for who they truly are. Without attachments or expectations they can grow into their power and vulnerability to be the part of the one organism they came here to be.

Purpose 6: Establishing New Societal Templates

The co-creation of Oneness and unconditional living and sharing goes beyond relationship in family. You will start co-creating a completely new world, based on a new source code/new templates that carry energetic signature of Oneness: Authenticity, compassion, freedom, responsibility, healthy interdependency, radical honesty, innocence, playfulness, living in the now are the basic ingredients for a new way for society to thrive and to live in harmony with nature and with each other. It will look very different from what we know and take for granted today. Everything will change, when it is no longer needed to satisfy ego needs of safety and power. When the human is valued instead of a currency. Arts and Beauty will have a revival to bring light into the world, to inspire and crack hearts open.

Economy will shift completely, and we will no longer need to exploit nature. Money, governments, democracy and linear hierarchies will be remembered as a bizarre phenomenon of the capitalist system. As each and everyone is going to return to full auto-responsibility, and back to following their emotional intelligence expressed in natural impulses and flow - there will be no need for someone taking control and take over responsibility for the collective. There will be nothing to fight or discuss about, as everyone is happy and appreciated for who they are and what they contribute.

THE ENERGETIC DYNAMICS

After having explored the purpose of a True Romance, we know what we are actually getting ready for. To understand why this process is so challenging and painful in the beginning, it helps to look into the energetic dynamics, the metaphysical perspective. This way, your mind has a chance to understand and start to support your journey instead of having endless drama loops.

Mirror Mirror

Your partner is your perfect mirror, mirroring back all of your fears, doubts, insecurities, and beliefs. It is his/her job! This connection is meant to empower you, and for that - all the old programming needs to go! It is too easy to slip into the victim role, to blame, to judge, to go into all the "he/she said" stuff, and to be focused on all the inadequacies and problems of the partner, judging their stuff they need to solve.

Scratch that. The sooner, the better. Unless you enjoy the push and pull dynamic and running and chasing game. It guarantees just one thing: This way you'll never reunite in a happy and healthy way, and the longing and suffering will just continue. So be brave and look into that mirror. Look at your own pain, your own patterns. Do your part. This prepares you to see the much bigger picture of Oneness. It is not just the partner you are one and connected with. He/she is just facilitating the access to a new world, where you see you are one with everything and everyone in this universe.

It Is All About You

Closely related to that is that we have to learn that it is always about us. And when we understand that we are one it makes sense, right? The more we shift, the more we inspire shifts for the partner and everyone. Nothing happens to us, everything happens for us. There is only US. And the faster you focus on yourself, on your own issues, your own healing, the quicker you raise your own frequency, and with it the frequency of the collective. You will feel much lighter and much more balanced than ever before. It helps to look into inner child empowerment and to learn more about metaphysics (you can find donation based video tutorials on my website thewakeupexperience.eu). This process pushes you to be and embody your essence, and strips away everything that you are not. It is triggering you until you have peeled off every conditioned layer and belief and have fully anchored in unconditional love for yourself and everything that IS.

The Spiritual Feminine Goes First

If you look at the process of creation explained with the running and chasing game in a previous chapter, you will get an idea of the dynamics, and why you - the carrier of the more spiritual feminine energy is first in this process. It is a given. If you wait for the partner to make the first move, you can wait until the cows come home. You are the one to come into embodied wholeness first, before they can actually start their process. The more you find your inner reunion and peace, the more they will feel the pull for change. A true reunion without a push and pull dynamic and endless triggers is only possible when both are fully embodied wholeness.

Silence Is Golden

It is very common in True Romances that there is an energetically forced separation and long periods of silence. This is actually a true blessing in disguise. Your transformation can happen a lot quicker if you are not permanently distracted by the presence of your partner. We are meant to transcend co-dependency, and the best way to do so is to do it alone.

Additionally, our body is not ready to be able to hold these high frequencies you share with your partner over extended periods of time. We would simply burn out with the friction between the emotional trauma and baggage we carry and the purity of unconditional love. So you do need those breaks in between to actually be able to align on a higher frequency band. The more you are able to recognize the gift of silence, the quicker you move through your own transformation. Focus on your own transformation instead of wasting energy on chasing and running away from your own lessons and job.

Your Inner Child Holds A Key

When you started our journey here on this planet, it did not take long until you were completely caught up in the game of duality (third dimension), and programmed with belief systems and templates of separation and lack. You took for granted what we learned. Everything was based on scarcity and competition and control. Being not good enough and having to be different, better. We did not question that maybe what schools, churches, governments, industries etc. told us was not so true after all.

You were wounded and hurt in early childhood already, because you were forced to compromise on your essence and uniqueness at a very early stage. Your fears and traumas that you experience today stem from that time. When you face a certain situation, your system recalls the memory of the past and reacts with the same strategy to get love and prevent pain that you have learned as a child. That results in anger attacks, crying, manipulating, pleasing, etc. You end up in the same mess again and again, until you realize that it is the pattern within you that keeps recreating these situations for you. Nobody is better at triggering your inner child than your partner. When the inner child is still in sabotage mode, it is the nurturer of the ego, feeding it the fear patterns the ego needs to stay in the lead. Our inner child needs to be empowered and experience unconditional love to transcend the pattern. This way, our ego needs to surrender and transform. And the only person able to provide that nourishing unconditional love is you!

Yay To Emotions!

Another big programming of duality is that acting out emotions is inappropriate and shameful. Crying, screaming, shaking, but also loud laughing or singing in public is considered to be inadequate. It seems odd that acting out emotions is a good thing and necessary!
It is a natural reflex that we have for a reason! It is like energetic puking. The purging is necessary to keep our system clean. Children naturally use that reflex. If they have an energy in their system that does not belong there, they scream, they cry or shake to release it right away. And everything is cool again a couple of minutes later. They are the role models!
Instead, we teach them that it is not okay to behave that way. So all of us keep all this toxic energy in our system and our emotional bodies get an overload up to a point of serious depression or physical pain and illness. And what do we do? We suppress it even further, take pain killers, alcohol and drugs to not have to deal with all that pain. Pain makes us even more cranky and snappy, and we become walking time bombs.

How crazy is that? Instead of blaming yourself when you feel emotional, turn it around and be grateful for the possibility to release it. This way, you learn to allow emotions constructively, without going into the drama.
Compare it with food poisoning. Your stomach reacts with the natural reflex to throw up. If you fight the reflex, you might get really ill or even die.
So - do yourself a favour and instead of judging yourself, enjoy the emotional releases with a big "Thanks that I can let this go now

for good." That transforms the energy and gets you out of a re-peating loop.

Start Sharing Your Essence

You don't need your partner to be an inspiring example of un-conditional love. Just start sharing your essence, your talents and gifts with the world. This is not about martyrdom, it is about what you love and what comes natural to you. This does not have to be big either. Redirecting your energy into purposeful cre-ations and acts of kindness are shifting your field!
Just remember that your "mission" is fun, and you thrive. If it is heavy and a lot of effort, it is not aligned with your essence.

3D School Was Necessary

In order to crack a system, you need to understand the system and all of its weaknesses. We needed to understand how the mind-matrix works so we could hack it, infect it, and inspire people to shift into the heart-grid. We needed to be able to relate to the pain and programming of people and experience ourselves how dual-ity feels like.

You Are A Transformer

During this experience, you become a true alchemist. You learn to transform energy from a low to a high frequency, by embracing and allowing, instead of trying and controlling. You learn that emotions, your vulnerability is actually your biggest strength, and the more you learn to process them constructively with gratitude and compassion instead of judgment and blame, the more you move into mastery of alchemy.

This way, you are transforming patterns of co-dependency, freeing yourself from the old matrix and its dynamics. True Romance actually prepares you to collapse co-dependency on a much larger level. The co-dependency with governments, with employers, with money, with health-care, with landlords etc. Once you can see co-dependent patterns, you cannot unsee them. You cannot see that all of them are based on conditions and conditional thinking. You can see that the human mind can actually only think in conditions, in cause and effect. If this.... then that. The mind projects a certain outcome based on expectations into the future, based on its experiences on the past. The mind cannot be in the NOW.

What is unconditional love and life then? It is presence in the NOW. It is the peace we feel with what is. It is loving everything as is. Nothing our linear mind can understand. Our heart knows, our emotional intelligence / our intuition knows. True Romance goes way beyond an unconditional love between two people. True Romance is a romance with EVERYTHING and EVERYONE. When we are able to be compassionate and unconditional with all that is, when we see and love the innocence in every human heart, no matter the mind programming, we have become a true master alchemist, and we create our reality based on pure, innocent love.
When we lead a heart based life, people around us shift into our vibration and are infected and inspired to remember their own wholeness and perfection. They are inspired to remember unconditional love. They remember that we are all One.

Your Life Was Supposed To Be Destroyed

This one is a very tough one to understand when coming from the mind that wants to do anything to keep us safe.
The love you feel is so strong that you would do anything to continue having it. Usually this craving for love involves the complete deconstruction of your old life and your co-dependent relationships.
This process is designed for you to bring you back to your true,

unique essence. That automatically means, everything where you have been compromising your essence is taken away. Any attachment you have is taken away. You will lose everything that you thought was important.

Your way of leading life turns around. From being driven by outside circumstances and people, to navigating with your inner compass. The realization that your energetic vibration is creating your experience. You are the one you have been waiting for! Everything you did to manipulate or control your outside reality is rubbed into your face until you surrender and let it go. Every mask you wore to hide your true essence is ripped off, until you stand naked in front of your very self. Until you realize this was the only real thing you ever had, and you start seeing your amazingness and your beauty. You start to see that the battle of darkness and light is really a battle that is taking place within you. Until you are loving your shadows unconditionally to transform them.

The more you fight, the harder it gets. You are tested many times if you truly trust the universal flow. This process frees you from everything that was holding you back. Holding you back from living the unconditional life you came here to live, together with other aspects of this beautiful human organism - people who have gone through that same transformation.

You discover the larger SELF, the human organism, and step by step, you get more glimpses of true embodied Oneness.

The art of alchemy is truly the key to your individual freedom and inner peace. In order to understand alchemy, we need to understand energy and energetic frequencies and dimensions.
In the chapter about the running and chasing phenomenon, you find the "Cycle of Creation", which contains a lot of information in just one sheet.

Alchemy is the art of transforming energy from one state of density to another. This does not necessarily refer to matter. In our experience of True Romance, we are talking about alchemy of feelings through emotion.

Different feelings have different frequencies. Fear based feelings such as disappointment, frustration, hate, unworthiness, etc. are of a lower frequency. They usually manifest as anger or sadness.
Love based feelings such as joy, playfulness, creativity, unity, appreciation, gratitude are of a higher frequency. They usually manifest as tears of joy, laughter and bliss.

When we look into the universal principles of metaphysics, the second law of thermodynamics states: Energy cannot be destroyed, it can only be transformed. How cool is that? That means, we can change the frequency of an energy!

How do we do that though when we are angry or depressed and sad? We start feeling and tuning into the feeling of a higher frequency. When we cry or are angry, we can start practicing gratitude that we can finally drop this weight and let it go. After some practice, we can go that far that we are actually joyful about the release, or redirect our energy into creativity. Music in certain frequencies (432Hz or 528Hz) can support you to find more ease. Treat yourself like you would treat an ailing friend in your situation. Take a bath, spoil yourself with a massage, or with

something that serves your well-being in that moment. Cuddle up with yourself.
Go out into nature, to align with the natural universal frequency of unconditional love. Watch children play to feel their innocence.

You will find your ways to transform your pain, simply by embracing and allowing it, instead of trying to control it, to fix it, solve it or block it. There is a big difference between drawing a line out of fear, or setting up boundaries out of self-love. When you catch yourself trying to protect or shield, you know you act from a fear-pattern not wanting to look at something within you that wants to be seen and transformed. A boundary is simply a clear "thank you but no" when something is not resonating with your essence. Discernment and self-observation is key.

The more you accept and see that everything you experience is your own creation, because it is simply an alignment with your own energetic frequency (synchronicity, law of attraction), the more you can embrace and be grateful for what is mirrored back to you, to point you towards what is blocking you from unconditional love, with the knowing that your reality will shift when you shift!

You will reach a tipping point, where life starts to give you some glimpses of fun again. As you move forward, bravely facing your deepest shadows, transforming them until no stone is left unturned, you will discover the beauty of aloneness. You need to be able to truly enjoy aloneness before you can actually be with someone or with more people in a completely new way. Not needing anyone, yet enjoying the company and togetherness as long as it lasts.

SEXUALITY

A big part of metaphysics is the sexual energy, and the difference between duality polarity and unity polarity.

In the third dimension (duality), we have encountered sexuality as a phenomenon that needs two people to be completely fulfilling, and it is a process triggered by the instinct of human reproduction. Sexuality is about hunting orgasms, property and possession, exclusivity, control and being controlled, etc.
It has many patterns of shame and guilt attached to it. No wonder! Because actually sexuality is the key to our biggest creative power.

It is therefore not uncommon that True Romance takes you into a longer period of a celibacy. It is needed so you can deprogram your sexual belief systems and discover completely new ways. A True Romance often triggers a Kundalini awakening, which is the awakening of the primal life force in your energetic system. It can get very uncomfortable when it happens, it feels like fire going through your energetic centers, burning away residue and clearing the system to be able to run life force (feminine) energy through you. The unconditional loving and nurturing mother energy is something to get used to!
It is not like it is switched on and from then on you are completely transformed, but it opens the door for you to connect more and more into the heart-grid, and unplug more and more from the mind-matrix.

In a first phase, you learn to truly explore and love and pleasure yourself to overcome any shame and judgment related to your body and being. You discover what you love, you start playing. You will probably experience random emotional releases when having an orgasm. That is a good thing! It is part of the cleansing to make space for new ways of sexuality.

In parallel, you might experience intense energetic sexual experiences with your True Romance partner, and you realize that distance does not matter. Nevertheless, be aware that this is still based on old duality principles, where you still feel the need for the other person to be fulfilled.

Your body, just like every human body carries a lot of sexual trauma, not only from your life, but from your whole family lineage, deeply stored in your cellular memory. This will show up for release. Situations will be presented to you that give you the chance to do so. Use discernment and follow your intuition, it is different for everyone. You don't have to jump into the bed with a self-proclaimed tantra guru, you don't have to go to dearmouring sessions, you don't have to be part of an orgie. It is not about forcing yourself, it is about playing and discovering, overcoming shame and guilt patterns. Be curious, explore, but also make sure you are in an environment where you feel completely safe and held, and where you can set up your own boundaries.

The more you transform sexual trauma, the more you open up to a completely new way of sexuality (unity polarity). It is no longer co-dependent, and no longer reaching or chasing something.
It is a full body experience of sexual energy that is running through you. Very blissful and orgasmic, yet very different from the orgasms we used to know. This energy is highly inspiring and creative, and brings you a beautiful flow.
You can have this experience with a partner or alone. You don't need any stimulation or penetration for it, it is simply the connecting forces within you of consciousness and life-force. The masculine and the feminine. When sharing this with a partner, it is even amplified.

This is what an inner reunion feels like!

THE BIG PICTURE

Your True Romance is the perfect bootcamp to strengthen your higher dimensional muscles and shifts you from fear to love, from mistrust to trust, and from control to surrender. It basically shows you that everything you ever believed to be true needs to be turned around by 180 degrees to remember love. Everywhere you feel resistence, is where you find the door into liberation.

This might sound totally insane in the beginning of your experience, when all you want is be with that person. It sounds crazy that you seem to be so important. And yet, you are!
I have written this book for you for exactly that reason! So you know that you are not alone. There are many others going through that same experience. I have coached hundreds of people with a True Romance, and my website has had millions of clicks. So yes, you are important, and yes, this is real!
You are so loved, and so held while you are going through what you are going through. We are all here with you, cheering you on!

The more you move forward, the more you can see and feel. You learn so much about yourself, about humanity, about the universe. You are preparing to share your individual magic with the world. You will know when you need to know.
The more you move forward, the more you will embody unconditional love, life and sharing. You will learn how to surf the waves, and you will get better and better at it. You will meet new people, you will be guided by synchronicities and little signs of confirmation the Universe (yourself in a higher dimension) is giving you so you keep going. You will realize that coincidence does not exist, and everything is designed and mapped out perfectly

for you. You will realize that it is all about you! For you to come home, to remember, to love, and to co-create a new paradigm with other brave love adventurers like you!

You will realize that life becomes very simple when you live from the heart and in the moment. Life lives you, life moves you, your intuition guides you.
We are all meeting in a new dimension, where we create a completely new paradigm together, based on unconditional love, which has literally nothing to do with anything we knew before. It is all perfectly orchestrated. No need to hurry, no need to try.

I am so looking forward to see you there!

LINKS

For helpful articles and tutorials on the process of awakening, on quantum physics, dimensions, inner child empowerment, realities etc. visit https://thewakeupexperience.eu

For information on the creation of a whole new paradigm for our human society, based on unconditional love, please visit and join us at https://ffmovement.org

ABOUT THE AUTHOR

Vera Mygdala

Vera is a loving rebel from the heart. She is trusting and following her inner impulses, wherever and to whatever she is called to. She intuitively understands and reads complex structures and systems. She is able to feel and see where the flow is blocked, and sees what is needed to unclog it. She has a natural and encouraging way with people, seeing and feeling their essence.

She is a true catalyst, and loves to create cognitive dissonances and AHA effects, by sharing new perspectives, and translating what is going on into simple down to earth language, usually with a good portion of fun in it. She looks back on a corporate career as Head of Communications in the automotive industry, before her whole life got turned upside down by a romantic soul encounter in 2014. After three years of life coaching and writing (thewakeupexperience.eu), she followed her renewed heart's calling - to create reference points of a new way for society.

Her childhood hero Pippi Longstocking keeps inspiring her way of life. She's living the true romance with her partner Agustí, and together they are creating fun and inspiring designs and blueprints, based on universal laws, data and codes, for a new way of living in a new world. They share a passion for music, art, quantum physics and universal magic, and they love to show what is possible beyond the thinkable. For more, visit ffmovement.org

Printed in Poland
by Amazon Fulfillment
Poland Sp. z o.o., Wrocław

65656001R00040